Marble

Contents

written by Julie Ellis

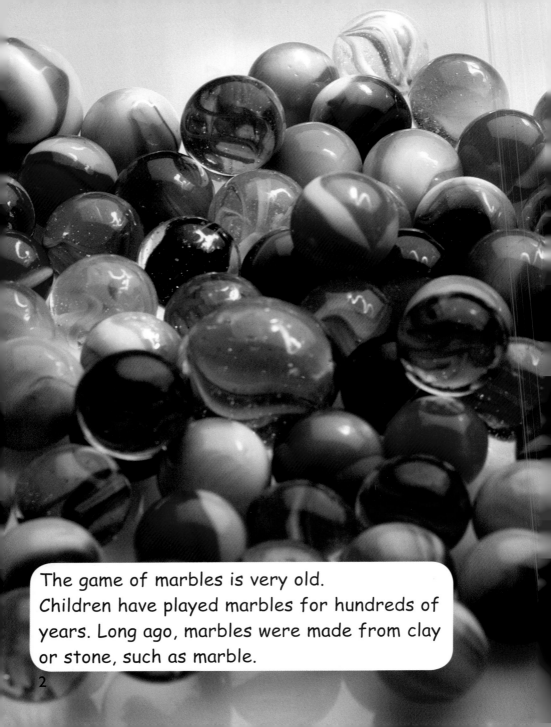

The game of marbles is very old.
Children have played marbles for hundreds of years. Long ago, marbles were made from clay or stone, such as marble.

Now, most marbles are made from glass in factories, but a few special marbles are made by hand. Marbles can also be made from wood, metal, agate, or steel.

There are many different kinds of marbles. When you are collecting, you could choose one kind, like glassies, or you could buy lots of different kinds. You need a marble bag to keep your collection safe.

You might choose to trade some marbles with your friends. Even though many marbles are made, they are all different. You are sure to have one special marble in your collection.

Marbles are named in different ways.
A "cat's eye" is named for what it looks like.
A "glassie" is named for what it is made from.
A "boulder" is named for its size.

How do you think these marbles were named: milkie, spotted, pee-wee, steelie, swirl, clearie?

There are different ways to shoot your marble. The first is called Knuckle Down. Keep your knuckles on the ground and flick out your thumb to push the marble towards the target.

The second way is by rolling, which is the easiest way. Just roll the marble toward the target. The third way is by flicking. Flick the marble with your longest finger.

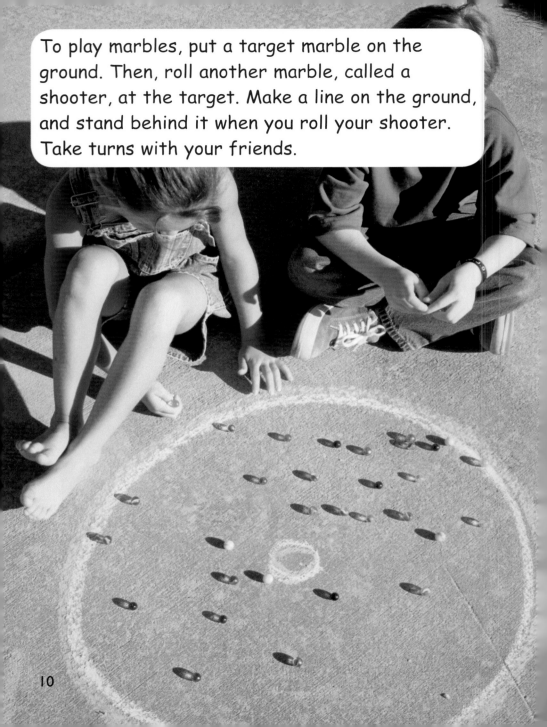

To play marbles, put a target marble on the ground. Then, roll another marble, called a shooter, at the target. Make a line on the ground, and stand behind it when you roll your shooter. Take turns with your friends.

If you are playing "keepsies", and your shooter marble hits the target marble, you can keep the target marble. If you are playing "friendlies", and your shooter marble hits the target marble, you must give the target marble back.

To play Ringer, put thirteen marbles in an X-shape in the middle of a circle. Players take turns shooting from outside the circle. The first player to knock seven marbles out of the circle wins.

To play Dropsies, one player tries to hit the other player's marble by standing over it and dropping a marble on it from eye level.

Lagging is a game where you draw a line on the ground and take turns tossing your marbles forward to hit the line without going over it.

Another way to play this game is to use a wall as the target. The winner is the one whose marble is closest to the line or wall without touching it.

There are many other ways that marbles can be used. They look pretty in a fish tank. You could use bright marbles to hold up flowers in a vase. You could have a competition to guess the number of marbles in a jar. Fifty? One hundred?